TEN-HEADED ALIEN

Also by David James Brock

TEN-HEADED ALIEN

DAVID JAMES BROCK

Buckrider Books is an imprint of Wolsak and Wynn Publishers.

Cover and interior design: Ingrid Paulson
Cover image: ©iStockPhoto/Gremlin
Author photograph: Anita Nagra
Typeset in Whitman and ITC Avant Garde
Printed by Coach House Printing Company Toronto, Canada

 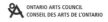 Canadä

The publisher gratefully acknowledges the support of the Canada Council for the Arts, the Ontario Arts Council and the Government of Canada.

Buckrider Books
280 James Street North
Hamilton, ON
Canada L8R 2L3

Library and Archives Canada Cataloguing in Publication

Brock, David James, author
    Ten-headed alien / David James Brock.

Poems.
ISBN 978-1-928088-55-4 (softcover)

    I. Title.

PS8603.R6225T46 2018   C811'.6   C2018-900524-6

THE POEMS IN THIS BOOK ARE...

53 PROG II: TEN-HEADED ALIEN

PROG I

GOOD MEN
GOOD RHINOCEROSES,
UNFORTUNATELY.
– EUGÈNE IONESCO,
RHINOCEROS

Tell Me What to Do (Now that I'm Awake)

Tell me which song, played first, will get me out of bed today.

Tell me if I'm simulating the general anxiety in the bass solo I heard on a
    subgenre album's twenty-eight minute track.

Tell me there's a prize for the losers in *Jeopardy* played to the death.

Silver medal. Pawn hearts. Blue ribbon. Brain salad.

I start this morning's tournament of champions down in the hole, a goblet
    of brain choir with a skull full of strings.

I'm burnin' for you under the patchwork quilt my mother sewed from the
    Fabutanned skin of my fake brother, Bailey.

March Madness. This or That. Kumite. Sixties Space Race.

I just woke from a dream where I was buying Cherry Skoal with a Discover Card
    in the Van Allen belt.

I blow hot air and alien metal into my bio because my name rhymes with
    Prog Rock.

Tell me where to watch tonight's moon set from a sober white cliff.

Waxing. Waning. Gibbous. Billy Gibbons.

Tell me the name of the tune the man in dandelion high-tops whistles
    as he Electric Slides up Yonge.

In the Leonard Cohen funeral fantasy, my friends hate me once they translate
    my boredom with Canadian eulogies.

Today is just a duded up klatch of *Either/Or*: baroque or proto-prog, Soho
    photobooth or Instagram selfie, either the rest of my life or the rest of my day.

An artist I admired traded in his name, his diet, and now offers tarot
    readings on Space Station Mir.

Today is an armadillo on wheels posing by an octuple rainbow.

Today is an arm transplant where the arm keeps choking you because
    your arm was the arm of a killer!

In a galaxy far from my electric light toothbrush, everyone had to get out
    of bed for the job they were given: trilobite chef, cyborg wet nurse,
    executive assistant to the necromancer of soldiers.

Tell me that mood is a genetic scheme, getting soused a gene and that
    back in the day life expectancy was πr-cubed

Tell me my wartime strategy would have been a hideout, a dreamboat
    oil rig off Crete, learning to play "The Bladder-Stone Operation"
    on a viol for a tuberculotic lover.

Tell me my post-nuclear strategy will be a soft rock party on an oil-can
    hoverboard.

Tell me my GMO-ragamuffins would hate the coward they saw in a
    water-stained black & white writing sonnets in a trench.

Double sunrise is an alarm clock singing *Robot roll call.*

Metallurgy: pre-beginner, and I spilled the molten nickels.

Fry a perfect platypus egg: one, and it was luck with a mindcrime of butter.

Autopen autographs: piss poor.

Servo. Gypsy. Crow!

What vinyl-loving prick of a friend taught me my binary habits through
   soundtracks?

Judgement Night. Xanadu. Astro-acoustic covers.

Tell me I'm superstitious, then get me three steel ladders, two spayed
   cats and whatever the witches in *Macbeth* needed.

Bubble. Trouble. Toil. Hubble.

Tell me that trivia will triple-drown this abraxas, pull the whip from his
   hand, drag my ass off the mattress.

It's only music, bro, pick a twenty-two-minute song and shimmy, says one of
   my McConaugheys forged in the land of the grey and pink.

Outside, I hear a two-headed spaniel bark.

I look out the window: no spaniel of Orthus, just a unicorn with its skin
   turned inside out.

I know you're out there this morning, in suits of armour, mittens over
   iron thumbs, -15°C in the RadioShack parking lot where they once
   held Viking funerals.

Tell me how much bitcoin's in my bank vault, so I can buy a castle on
   the butthole surf.

Krapp's tapes. Mixed tapes. Tapes from FM-radio tapes.

Rambling VoxBox, bad choices, the guilt I felt draining my tattoo ink in
   the Phalasarna sun where I hoped to dry out.

Siri, tell me the Greek word for a brick thick man-baby?

Tell me where my tongue goes when I try to pronounce liver enzymes
or Cretan dishes on a menu?

I double-check phone-Twitter for strategic-retweet-opportunities.

My voice wolfs our air, your smart fridge, this white space . . . *mic drop!*

My therapist's disembodied head tells me, *does this music decision really
matter —play all the songs*, motherfucker.

Your thoughts are the things in your way, motherfucker.

Enter the ring with me, motherfucker, says the Axl Rose who won't sue me.

Tell me to write a poem called "Someone is Always Telling You Not
to Worry."

Tell me to write a novel like Hardcastle or de Mariaffi.

Tell me to write a play like Moscovitch or *Betroffenheit*.

Tell me to learn backflips or comet-riding or enjambment.

Today I will lie to everyone I see: *I read that book too. I know all the stars
in Draco. I'm fine, and you?*

So it's hot-or-not to the streaming service finalists: *Yes* (1972) or
Marin Marais (1792)?

Contrabass. Roundabout. Mellotron. Harpsichord.

Tell me to stop scrolling through music and 3-2-1 the morning's mute
button.

Tell me to be bad and bold and wise and stronger, so I can hold up Roy
    Halladay's plane from the Gulf of Mexico.

Tell me to drink red punch mixed by the Blue Öyster Cult, to control a
    cottage fire, to keep the most beautiful griefs from a stage.

Tell me I'll be, like, dead by 2112.

My drink of choice is a happy hour bucket of Harold on the rocks.

I haven't told anyone what I mean for a super-duper long time.

"Aqualung," "Motorbreath," "21st Century Schizoid Man."

Tell me which one.

"Shitlist," "Limelight," "Linoleum" – "Get in the Ring" is in my head.

I'm in a terrible place for an odyssey to start.

Just tell me which one.

I've been awake for ten seconds.

This is just how the days start right now.

Tell me which song to play.

Bionic Pigeon Wing on the Roadside

There's this single wing synthesis, just one part left
from the bionic pigeon. The curb is thick with road dust
and titanium bones retain their shape. Red wires

spit sparks to signal *It's over*. And maybe the rest
of the fleshmachine is in the scrap heap, molted and sold
per pound. Maybe the automaton flies in circles with just

one wing, searching, programmed for searching, a lost
piece of self. Or maybe each part has found its way. Brain
of silicon in a coder's trophy case. Heart of palladium

and tantalum among the taxidermist's shelves. The cryolite
eyes become playground marbles in games of keepsies
where the runts learn to gamble. Maybe the other wing,

also broke from body, is halfway up the road, carried
a klick in the gutterwind the 191 makes. Or this: the second
wing sleeps in a street sweeper's belly. For now, we have

one wing levitating in pulses of traffic's breath. We can't find
the rest of it. But it could only go so far without closed
loops of the intact machine. These blood-and-guts birds

have no mystery. They die in heaps at clean glass windows.
They evolve pygostyles when tails impede flight. Lop off
that parson's nose of cooked birds. Our birds learn tool use

and puzzles. Their feathers drop from high-voltage lines,
free from forged deaths our created wings cling to. *Don't look*,
we say – then look. Recoil at their mess. Bionic pigeons spare

us roadkill. They leave us nothing. We are left searching for
a lost piece. And maybe a crow perches on a doorknob, picks
a lock with an artificial ulna. Cracks the door and drops the key.

Sunrise with Sea Monsters

You'll love my children more than I do.
I will brag about a sapphire dug

from the sandbox. You'll think I'm
hungover. Gin. I am, and I'll have kid shit

in my fingernails. A night swigging art
is a hulk eschewing the shore, but the

swimmer is poor, sighs then sinks.
· ·

Dumb tentacle slaps the single parent:
a detriment . . . only two eyes watch . . .

Compare it to a pirate lost in a gulf.
Half ♂ vs. a four-eyed leviathan.

Compare it to the one-armed ♀
juggling her bully boys. Go on. Pump out

new cowards who fear the stone they turn to.
· ·

You'll hate this. Fires blind the

coastal fabric stitches. DNA and dental
records are ash. I sketch my dad strong

with Poseidon's head: ψ.
Drag phobias to the water column's

lowest part. Here is where a
sea god bobs, a body mishmash birthed.

balloon Balloon BALLOON

Six: Robot chooses blue from a carny.
It is only kind of like the blue of sky.
Carny loops ribbon 'round wrist yaw, and Robot fears her own liftoff.
The countdown stops when Robot remains planted.
She reads her gravity.

Five: the Ferris wheel is a robot.
The Tilt-a-Whirl is a robot.
The popcorn machine and helium tank are robots.
She reads her motion and material in their order of clank and hiss,
       while the balloon goes squirmy on her wrist.

Four: now she watches the balloon amble up into the blue…blue forever.
Escape is a glum dance.
No program can retrieve the balloon.
Complex language cannot retrieve the balloon.
Robot reads knot as ally, knot as balloon saviour.
A clown says, *No more blue, but there are plenty of orange, little boy.*
Robot reads that all is lost forever.

Three: twenty minutes later, a popped blue balloon sways to Earth and
       lands mute without much opera.
A worm rests upon the blue, and a gull finds the worm in the grass.
Violence comes at the carcass of the blue balloon.

Two: in four days, the worm-eating gull is eaten by a gull-eating gull.
The meal cries.
Bird tears are a shrill song, rare though.
The blue balloon is now litter, unmoved and forgotten.
A dead balloon.
Nothing else now.

One: Robot is kept awake by floating thoughts.
She reads loss as blue balloons on the moon, planted by the astronaut
    who didn't make it home.
She reads loss as a field of blue looking for wind.
Loss as a lonely spaceman on moon prairie, singing anthems of
    one-way trips.

Offers More than Earthly Meat and Drink

The Soprano is Offered a New Liver for Her Voice

She's not a mermaid. This isn't
a punishment for stealing fire.
The offer: *keep song or cirrhosis.*
The eagle doesn't rest at night.

This isn't a devil's pact. She keeps
soul – though she offers it. *No,
this is my offer: live or sing?*
The terms are plain and grim.

The bargain will break chains,
not a hero. Not an axe, and not a
drug. She has a choice. *Trade your
gift and live or stick around silent,*

but stick around. The slow villain
comes around, then turns away rejected.
It's a little test to think about, a last
breath soon, or later, silent?

The Composer is Offered Height for His Ability to Compose

How tall do you want to be? Just three
inches more. He wants to see the world
from the height of the lighting grid.
The applause climbs on opening night's

success. This isn't the story of a composer
spiking a rival's wine with strychnine.
There were no rivals, but a tall man who
once walked down Sauchiehall with a beautiful

woman. The composer instantly loved her
in his mind. If she could hear his music, he
thinks she would love him. But she won't,
so he wishes to be tall. *Are you ready?*

Just say the word. The composer bites.
He has grown and lost a shadow. They will
love him for another reason now, and who
are you to judge? Who claps when you stand?

We each get a little test, and that test
should not treat us like a toy
between divines at war. We mistrust
ironic punishments: too perfect.

The chiropractor, for example, almost never
loses her hands. The birdwatcher isn't
blinded by sun at the peak of the swallow's
flight. The eyebrow cocks towards the

hippocampus doubting the banker gone
broke or cops cuffed to bunk beds in
cages. Time lapse shows the dead fox as
compost. It's finally cruel when the dancer

is told of a slow slip inside the myelin
sheath. *I can save you, but you will turn
tragic.* The grizzly lurks at the river, so
the salmon jumps into its gentle teeth.

Identifying Voice Type by Sneeze

Basso profondo of the blue light bus bragging,
I can tell a stranger's voice by that stranger's
sneeze. He dreams of allergy season, *all that*

tessitura spewing out on public buses. Can I
tell you a secret? The secret's not in the Ah . . .
it's all in the Choo. We quiet, all of us,

waiting for the next stranger to reveal
herself on the blue light bus, and it's so so late,
we miss our stops, and we worry, it will never

come, and the wait slows the bus to a crawl,
so we concentrate. Concentrate. Concen –
A woman sneezes . . . *Gesundheit!* We willed that

together, and he exclaims, *Mezzo-soprano!*
We believe he's done it. Strangers hug on
the blue light bus. I shake a prophet's hand.

Narcissus, Shiny Bar, Echo

Narcissus's hand is palm up this afternoon, resting
supplicant, fingers bent like tree roots beneath
pavement, the crack in the sidewalk is admirable
resurrection, a nature versus man conflict
on a home's façade. He begs for nothing, this is just
how the freehand rests on the bar. The bar top
is scuffed from similar moments of self-reflection –
knocked on by rings and watches, carved by Camaro keys.
Somehow the past always divines an empty stool in
a dark bar. Ass pockets loaded with quarters.
Femurs jammed into creaky acetabulums. There's no
song on the juke for soundtrack. He hides from a world
not looking. Hides from the contagion of superficial
laughs and knows why he has so few friends
to preach some truth. He isn't quite unhappy.
He only hears his own voice in his own head in his
own GPS location. It's one p.m. and maybe the day won't
improve. A woman with gout walks in, and he knows
the statue he carves is not an image anyone could love.
But he could love her after Hello. He says, *Hello.* She says
nothing, which he takes as surprise. This was a big
scene in the booze-can picture. She takes a seat
at the opposite end. Her name is Echo, he'll never
learn it, and only he can see her palm flop up.
As if a mirror between them breaks by new roots,
and a trunk thrust up through bottles and dust.

My Head Becomes a Cadillac Escalade

and the stereo kicks, so you like me better.
You can't blast Van der Graaf Generator tunes
with the head of a Cadillac Escalade. It defeats
the purpose of a Cadillac Escalade for a head.
You can play Chance & Drake & Gaga where my
opinions on politics once were. I can get you
from A to B if A is where you are and B is where
I'm going. My legs need some time to adjust to
the new weight. A factory model is 5,800 pounds.
As your kids grow, my hammies adjust. One day
everyone piles in after a party and my legs
can barely handle the freeload, but I'm wearing
my PUMA Clydes, so here we go. I drink premium
gas. Stop talking to me while you're filling up.
I can't hear you so good with that nozzle in
my ear. Other than that, things aren't so different.
I've kept my mesomorph frame, just now my
head is a Cadillac Escalade. Things have been
much worse. The whole bar would kill to have
a Cadillac Escalade for a head. I just got lucky.

Woman with the Head of a Fish in Parkdale

Woman with the Head of a Fish tumbles
upstream, a school of mermaids grace past,
white locks flow, caudal fins bob while Fish
beholds a mob of satyrs primping onshore.

In sweeps manticore to pluck Fish for lunch,
but he smells a taste he won't digest, moves on
to meal the baby ashrays – who still don't know
that the light will melt them. Fish wriggles

and hopes her screams can drain the quag –
grindylows tickle her belly. She begs for salve
or lover or cure, begs for guillotine or filleting
myths. This river wasn't always chewing gum,

her legs were once nimble, elegant for the run,
but this strip overwhelms its deviations.
Now a pox keeps Fish from leaping out.
The bunyip, that dog-faced echinoderm, lurks.

Scylla thrashes all six skulls on the banks.
White water is not a symptom, the bottom
rocks are muggers, the sun is napping in
the rotten west, so Fish swims east.

I Only Eat What I Kill: Volume 1

I shot its neck while it sipped from a pink
and fast stream. I approached the kill
for field dress, and pressed my sharp knife
at its stagnant windpipe. No blood
at the bullet, none in the snow,
no blood when I cut through the fur.
Just clockwork at the trachea,
mainspring in the mandible, spring
and ratchet at the gut of the tongue.
A savoury flashback makes my mouth ache.
I will die of starvation looking
at a *Made in Switzerland* tag.
Snow falls as crystals crushed from
quartz clouds imagined in prototyping.

Obituary for Old Moon

Old Moon withdrew from orbit. Only Greek gods, long deserted,
could've built a useful tether.

Old Moon beelined for Mars, left it be and bonked around the asteroid belt.
She saw Ceres and Vesta, Hygeia, Pallas . . . then disappeared among
Jupiter's spheres where it wasn't the only one called *moon*.

Telescopes got over it. Earth eyes grew bored with night perpetually in
no moon.

Artificial Moon® was launched, a proprietary formula duplicated Old Moon.
A.M.'s engineers were new lunatics.

      Ω   Love song lyrics were rewired.
      Ω   *E.T.* was yanked from the Library of Congress.
      Ω   Armstrong and Aldrin were wiped from the lexicon.

Our wallowing in the abandonment ceased in a single cycle.

There was once mystery in the sky, a rock lit white by Old Sun.

We saw it all, then stopped looking.

Our symbolism watched us while we slept.

Old Moon watched us leave her long ago.

GRUNGE

SOME PEOPLE EAT CARS.
– ANNIE DILLARD,
THE WRITING LIFE

Flatbed of a Dozen Pigs

That flatbed was late for delivery, and the pavement died at the shoulder.

We were torpid on the parquet floor as though we'd rained from the ceiling.

A room of people I wanted to love forever brought rum and weed.

We were full on ham too sweet and briny with booze and mustard.

The twelfth suckling was wedged in the wooden slats of the flatbed and lived.

She was walked from the scene, slow on a leash to the slaughterhouse.

We all watched *Paint Your Wagon* – I rubbed feta cheese on a honey-baked ham.

We all wanted a little more salt and sugar or rum and coke and time.

I haven't eaten pork since an orphan Easter about that week when a pope died.

The brakes locked, and the truck flipped ass over nose to the moon.

Eleven Berkshire sucklings took air, and gravity called them back to Earth.

I Love the Laser

I love the laser that kills the man in the first
minutes of the movie. I love the laser's boom.

I love the elephant ivory grip of the laser held
at the cowboy's thigh. He didn't know he'd kill

The Fox today – with the laser – but there is
pink blood in the dirt of a Mexican cantina.

There is a laser in the backdrop of the sunset.
There is a blue eye taking aim from the back of the

laser's barrel. The casings clunk on the horse
trough's oak. A man's skull is deleted over yonder,

and the undertaker titters. I love the rumoured
laser that shut down an animal phys exam in '99.

The laser that was sold for a tasty profit in the
pawnshop. We are on the hunt for lasers to kill

the ten best terror boys. Lasers that kill a reporter
and a cameraman live! That fit in the wide receiver's

sweatpants' pockets, that steal a Slim Jim or a pack
of darts, whisk apples from heads without singeing

single hairs. But then, I fired lasers at beer cans, begged
Pal to bury the photographic evidence. How murders

are covered up, let alone the death of a Coors can,
is an A&E nooner mystery. *Come on, Pal. A laser in hand*

will kill my rep. I feel no little pang of guilt when the
8-bit duck explodes, when Bambi's mom dies, when

someone calls the knife a man's way to bite it. A kid
gets shot and cooked through the throat in a movie and it's

labelled a comedy. I can't cry in the face of each laser
pointed directly at me. *Psych!* They ain't pointed at me.

The laser is a god's gift. So go on, give lasers to
teachers and students, priests and believers, sinners

and pilots, one secret passenger. The plane cruises
at thirty thousand feet, no one aims up, and we sleep all right.

BC Interior

Buddy lands the Cessna hammered. He's lax on the rules
covering his pilot's licence. He runs the case of empties from
fuselage to thorn bush 'case the cops show. Once in the clear,
we laugh our grit sore and pass bottles by firelight.

Goon thinks we're subjects of a manhunt, but our crimes
stay unseen. We refuse to reveal our evils. We learn from
elders to hog-tie screams in the midsection where
bad cancers live. Now is the quiet part of our adventure,

and there are killer plots among the crickets. We're each
family men and assassins. Release mind sausage. We're
too old to mix *rage against* with *make love, not war*.
A candle with no flame is not a symbol. Time writes

autobiographies better than any pen, and the bargain with
clocks is a sword flailing at crab stars. Back on Earth, we
learned surfing while sitting on lawn chairs at concrete
driveways near no oceans. We read the right rags, sent

doppelgängers to be toes to the nose on the tube. It's a
poltergeist that forever carves the waves, and all bodies
are swept up in the undertow. Drown power hides the splash.
We repeat power to remember power. We see power

in a puddle jumping from gutters off truck tires. We see
the child drenched at a crosswalk. Her party dress is ruined.
Our party is the cyclone. Our origin story is ruined in lies that slip.
But what romance isn't ruined? We didn't die at twenty-seven.

We mistreated our lovers and children. We aren't prodigies,
and our parents did not get their wish. Their parents did not
get their wish. Another lie was the aggressive life. No one
sanded our edges. We hate these endings, but we have them

coming for each haphazard act. An ending is always coming.
Our heroes die before us and take an image with them. We
forgive them. We are no one's hero, and our checklists have
empty boxes. Lou goes, *Will we be talked about when we're*

gone? Padre goes, *We won't be mourned.* We fear that
our hearts will be autopsied for their lack of kindness, that
a beast in the chest will be found. So we pledge to forgive
everyone on their deathbed if we ever loved them once.

Sky Ghoul

Toil while we only look in light for answers.
Interstellar dark. Villains in the cracks.
Culprits missed and distraction conjured.
We can't see creatures in the stars
that aren't the stars – we're ignorant of
the sky ghoul's spectacle in a disappearance.
There was no wind or rain that day. Fire
never touched the girl, and a belt of stars
brewed above. Her mother's cry is apparition.
Nightview: Orion, black mountains, fire blanket
on Pacific canyon, rust and a vigil. Some walls
are deeper sky-high. Flames are immigrants
feared. Flames crawl up America-side, lungfish
learns amphibian. Port Angeles cooks and burns.
The fires

cross borders.
The search party's props are horror-story standard.
Map and bloodhound and flashlight – her crusty
photo foretells a child gone missing, as if her eyes
looked to loud fates in a crystal ball. *My girl*
(the mother) *have you seen her?* While sparks
tiptoe off Canadian shore rock, Dallas Road side,
where *We'd just come to see the shipwreck.*
Blowtorch armies put candles on that old
flatboat. The mother ages by the waves.
She keeps watch at the barge, just scrap metal
beached at the stones near the hot view
states-way. No one breaks: from firewalk,
work order, hand on shoulder. Embers flit,
fake fireflies, some soft kindling to escape the
global tent. A ghost knows who to blame for
the girl who floats away as the sky goes crazy.

Dear Straw Men,

Shhhhh. Put the straw to your lips.
Breathe through the straw. You are

buried. This isn't pleasure, but
you have punishment lust. So we

bury you alive in the ejectamenta.
You're isolated talents, Sisyphean buds,

and we bury you in shit. Don't writhe,
you are the hill, not the rock. But

we're not monsters, honest, so
here's the straw. See? Mercy.

This straw is a lifeline. Contemplate,
while you live in shit, the lightning rod.

Admittedly, an image for thesis: the
lightning doesn't climb the roof, steady

up the shingles and point at victims in the
yard. The lightning was here first. Listen.

We'll pop two straws in your earholes,
so you don't miss the skinny. You know

these straws are protean. Your premise
is compost, so fields might grow here.

Take the straw. Come on, take it. We'll
meet halfway. Shortly, I'll pop a straw

in my own gob. Quick demo. You can't
talk with a straw in your mouth.

Just breathe, fellas. You'll live. You're lucky.
You have the straw. I'm offering you

the straw. The best cure for *wrong* is *learn*,
the best salve for mean spirit is burial

in shit. So now you're buried in shit.
Learn to relish the Ceremony of Straw.

The lung tunnel. It might terrify you,
the number of secret straws in pockets,

the smothers on a daily basis, friends
with straws as knife and shield and parachute.

So, I necropsied a rodent, punctured its
organs (an act of love) and the bile

stung my hand. Invasions, their choleric
grace, stink like temperature. You're right.

We do have shovels. Maybe we will
dig you out. And you're right, we have

mobs and pitchforks too. But, I'll go
this one solo, so we both can jerk ourselves

to gladiator fantasies after, with the straws
in our mouths. Slowly now, here's a bendy,

a fun one. Take this straw as a finger
pressed to lips. Shhhhh. No. Shh.

I Only Eat What I Kill: Volume 2

Southwest grazing plains, this time zone induces terror.
Intimidate me, wild boar. The spectre of an extinct
food supply remains. We all know the ghost of bison roam.

Welcome to the hamlet of Void (population: fluctuating).
Sunrise comes earlier than it used to, don't it? The Earth
is a big meat aisle in the plaza, the run is on.

Beast eats man, raven eats tiger body. Tomorrow's meal
has insomnia tonight. It dreams lightning, foot fast
and free of the snare. Your entire genus will be eaten.

Dead fresh while buzzards live high on the hog. Waste
a morning in a food hangover. Lethargy is the sound of bread
sopped in gnu skin gravy. Black eye bags, heavy lids.

Thirsty. Bring water, please. I am drowning from outskirts
to insides, my guts are stew of subprime ingredients.
It's not rock bottom until we eat our machines.

What really is the difference between enzyme and scream?
Both are present at a breakdown. My sickness wins till lunch.
Let's eat and eat like our food pulses, eludes us.

The kill will surely fight back one day. I am ready with rifle,
knife and spices. If I pull out my teeth, one by one, will you
finally trust me? Just come closer. I promise this is not a trap.

Please help, I'm at the edge of the world this morning

where the spiders outweigh me.
I'm trespassing the Esquimalt shipyard.
The colours of pressed junked cars
stacked and bright. A grey cloud
is messy behind the metal like
mixed moods on a painter's palette.

There's an old tug on asphalt
that will never again see water.
There are already things done
for the final time. A choir of yawns
lingers. The hands that built
inactive ships are aura now.

The fish smell is just sea kelp
and garbage. Bird call enters. I'm dumb,
got shakes, don't know the song.
I'm the coast's scarecrow. No one look.
I swallowed two pills last night,
found in a friend's daughter's laundry.

The first pill made us laugh. The second
knocked me flat. I still wear last night's
clothes and boots, craving sunglasses
to block the assault. Dogs prowling
off-leash. Baby skin glowing sunburnt.
Beautiful joggers sweating by me.

Now block the motorboat screaming
in the harbour, now someone's ex
crying at a morning breakup. Now block
crackpots crushing tall cans under foot
and bald eagle's flight. Block the taste
of batteries on the back of my tongue.

Now the skater rattling walkway stones
near napping lovers on the sands
by the waves. Block hard geology.
A day moon up in the sky's blue gel.
Block that chimeric rock. I've wasted
so much beauty. Focus, man.

Focus on the fat squirrel darting
across path pebble. Watch it close.
Eagle eye it. Trace its angles. It flees
to the ocean, cascades off the cliff
like a lemming. Is it rumour – lemmings
careening from the scenery? Because

I'm at the edge of the world this morning. Please help.

the little punks have always counted

the little punks have always counted on a faith in
wishing wells, mouths of babes, a fear of dogs and
wolves, a trail of bread crumbs to the fire that boils
the witch's skin. they do a staggering amount of
coping lately. the little punks on migration routes,
yelling grievance in the winds. they drink molotov
cocktails now. so the little punks breathe fire at all
paperwork. bedtime fairy tales were stored in the
little punks' brains from the time those brains were
mush. emperors can still be naked and jailed *because
in the long run, the character of* the little punks
demands that kings be punished. if the pigs who
used straw and twigs lost their shelter, it is obvious
to the little punks that their weapon is the brick. the
little punks poison all the apples, shatter glass
slippers with those bricks. and too, the beanstalks
are property of the little punks. *a country is the sum
total of the character of its little punks.* take the little
punks seriously. they were children once and now
again. can i please be a little punk? they hide axes in
each mattress. the little punks are coming. so can i
join? can i be a little punk, too? no one sleeps when
a little punk counts.

the little punks have   faith
                                    fear
                                the fire
                        a staggering amount of

            grievance   they drink

paperwork.
                                those brains were
mush.

                                    it is obvious
                                            the
little punks   shatter

            the little punks.

                        were children
                        little punk?
                    little punk
                                no one
            counts.

Jake, Damien, Soft, Tender

Damien is stuffed in Jake's sack
after four fingers of brown. Jake's
daughter hates Jake. Jake slings
Damien over his shoulder on his way
to a dark match, the way Carthaginian
fathers bring a dead boy's body
home from a battle won. In the downtime,
Jake battles demons, while Damien sits
in glass cases sucking muscle from
Rattus norvegicus dropped in.

Damien heard Jake pin the Ugandan
Headhunter, heard grunts from a burlap
bag beneath the turnbuckle. Jake
battled demons in a quart of Jack:
Jake-drinking-Jack. On another night,
Damien was pimped out on a salty loser:
ko'd Calgarian's meat-stink-sweat.
Damien died, and was replaced by a
dead ringer. Maybe Damien One choked
on a hamster treat of *Mesocricetus auratus*.

Maybe Damien One starved, or was
just like Mama Cass, who didn't choke
on a ham sandwich, but like other creatures –
with a weakened heart: "Words of love,
soft and tender," won't keep Damien One
alive, anymore. Push Damien Two as
the official *Python molurus* of *Superstars*.
Jake's seed still hates Jake. Jake is no
dad of hers. He uses the brain as a
prop, drinks himself to jitters (ᴅᴅᴛ).

Witness the crippling of Jake, a limbless
anaconda without the grit. Jake put
Damien Two through all the grunt work.
Look at the famous Papa, and picture
him shiver. His muscles crave venom,
or wish they could squeeze life from
no-names, push souls out their navel.
Replace that father early, before
old mega man wins, wraps out
the air, and tightens, coils ... tightens.

Study the Universe and Reveal the Reason
Optimists Stopped Searching

On the occasion of the inauguration of the forty-fifth president of the United States

Yet we look for it with map and torch in every corner:
our search takes us to new beds, old bars. We look
under patriotic rocks and see pill bugs scavenging,

feeding on their own shit for the copper. So we go
underwater, to hot vents where the secrets mount, where
copepods thrive in impossible dark. We chase our big

kills. Endangered species. Meat. The brag of the hunt.
It's not a freedom we miss, but a loss of comfort
near our rarest carcasses. All joy is faux. No

gods ever presided. We're out of little guys to kick.
Don't say we didn't look. We whirled. Old logic
implied we'd get what we worked for. That was super

childish. We congregated, repeated *We'll be okay*. We
kid ourselves with pep rallies. We leave each other
wounded. It was gobbledygook that a common good

annuls specific evil. The fables are a typo. Rocks reject us.
Deep, so deep, a squat lobster smiles in its cozy blindness.

Some Monsters Live as Jewels

When it falls off, I'll make earrings of
your toenail hematoma. I want that blue
stone. I am soaking bones at home. I've
carved wedding rings from ring fingers,
but those lovers didn't last. A necklace
of tendon hangs near a broken heart.
I've framed tapestries of ink and skin,
taut, hacked lockets from kneecaps.
I wear an amulet of my mother's ankle
bone, so she can still protect me. The
Merlot swell must burst from your toe,
your body will decorate a body. I want
to bite it, release the burden in your foot.
Your magic reminds me of my brooch,
jewel-set in a tranquil vampire's tooth.

Newfoundland II

Build an island of litter, update borders
of the fibreglass globes, Sharpie® new shapes

on all the flat maps. WAGE PEACE and wait
for volcanoes where the outrage can spew,

pray the lava is carbonated and good
in glass bottles. Or melt the bottles, erect the

pellets as war memorials: there's drama
when soldiers might shatter. Put the first

bird that lands on our shore in the new
nation's flag. REMEMBER THE LAVA. Let it destroy

weak parts to make canyons: we will need
wicked beauty to look at while gardeners

work the moon. Get that flag bird in the meat
of our national dish. Support your local sculptor

who reminds us of the farmer's former charm.
IT'S YOUR DUTY TO LITTER. SUSTAIN THE LAND.

Donate to photographers who capture carcasses
in matte: a sea otter's bones sheathe Fanta® can

flotsam, and give us our fancy coat of arms.
ACT NOW, CITIZENS. No need for more words.

Someone is *Always* Telling You Not to Worry

It happens anyway, these worries. Asteroids miss
the Earth by parsecs sometimes. Predictions
for the end of the world are fifty-fifty. Who bears life looking

for meaning in flat tires on abandoned cars in sagebrush,
expiry dates on dairy products atop Formica dining tables.
Someone you love cannot wait for you, but you only

interpret this when you scratch your initials on carbon
paper to imagine simple life: '70s contracts, onions
in an order when I said no onions or *Sold* signs on

the dream home lawn with mom and pop who must just
laugh as they did when they still fucked in their twenties.
Now the three-year-old and five-year-old flop from some

sensible truck. I go jealous that they are startling.
Who can take this bombardment, tin rain on tin roofs,
faith in failure as a rolling jewel in a bathroom sink?

Disco's Out, Murder's In

We're not meant to dance, the knee joint
barely bends for it. Our hands are built
cruel in the shapes of knife handles, or two
hands the right size for all sorts of choking

horrors. Trigger complements finger as if
both are sex organs born in primordial soup.
We are cocaine desperate to see honeybees
boogie oogie oogie. Bird display is nightclub

lust. Our best attempt at feathers appear as
psoriasis on the elbows. We have a history in
the helix to follow fear. Some movements are
insignificant: check mark in a bubble, the final

speck in a sentence. But the tapping toe in a
police lineup reveals each new guilt. We blame
biology for cool violence. Our simplicity is clean
choreography, the backlash is a hot mutant baby.

Curse of Superman

Teach the little green men of our actors
      their unemployment, Alzheimer's,
            clots that jam veins and end

a spin around the globe.
      Show them abuse, the short
            flight from infant to teen death –

huffs of solvents meant to get us high,
      to lift us up, up,
            but only steel us away. Bring little

green men to gunshot murders
      staged as suicides, affairs shaping
            death tableaus. Get them to the man

falling from show horse to never walk
      again, let them stand by while quiet
            heart attacks rip out heroes

without regard for looks. Bear them
      witness each cause of death.
            We don't have an Achilles heel.

We are made of them.
      Kryptonite is a symbol for all susceptibilities.
      Have the little green men see that

we are not afraid of dying
      habits. We wear them on our chest.
            Preoccupy them with our curses.

Lie to them. We need protection.
      We're on the quest for superpower.
            We need to be invincible now.

PROG II: TEN-HEADED ALIEN

MOSTLY IT *WAS* SPACE. SO MUCH SPACE.
I LIKED THE IDEA OF NOTHING ON TOP,
NOTHING ON THE BOTTOM, AND A LOT
OF NOTHING IN BETWEEN, AND ME IN
THE MIDDLE OF THE NOTHING.
– RAY BRADBURY, "NO PARTICULAR
NIGHT OR MORNING"

Head One (Voice)

Submit and you won't get hurt, friends. The first
head is its concept of our voice, in every language, and
the other nine nod in agreement. They've read our bodies.
Learn and copy. Look at its body of obsidian ingot, biology
stolen from another space and clock. Save joules, shrink,
we must now be very small. I'm hiding, are you? Each head
is unique, but none so disembodied as our bum ideas.
Each head sways in colony like sea bottom vegetation
at home in the benthos. It must read that it needs
a single throne and ten gold crowns. The rest of our
calcium. Will we call it *They*? Will it leave princes?
What's king after cancer? Head One ignores our boring
needs for translation, our occupation history – ballistic
verbs don't work on its sensory systems. **I talk
in a frequency you sifted, friends.** Head One is mouthpiece,
vessel for masters backstage on some other star's rock.
Our evolved ears permit its tiny fucking fears. Doom,
death, our dead. **Bury yourselves and you won't get hurt,
friends. Doubt this? I've got silence.** In basso profondo,
it mega-arias toward our fate. **You want to negotiate,
but we're a mission hammer.** Ingot. Biology giant. Bad lyrics.
Nine other brains. **Receive us? Are you ready, friends?**

a Bracatus *Majoris:* Vox

Three will be sent to stop it – to be the cure

to the plague of the Super Duper that stone cold busted the 'burbs.

Who we thought we were was dollar store quality

beneath a biomimetic paw. We only jimmied the word for *home*

once we lost it. The Super Duper ripped labs

from floor plans, shouldered skylights off the roof.

Foundation was rubble. Bedrooms oozed blood in the

brutal extraction. The Goliath's lack of laser

precision made it a wilderness impossible to hack.

The Super Duper skulked, exfiltrated, clawed moon craters

in our soil. It competed with comet and malware, war and pestilence,

I-Worm.ZippedFiles, and the other alphanumeric horsemen.

Data was made into algorithm…men swan dived from skyscrapers and sat

for analysis. Single spots, making new stars in old graves.

Head Two (Trees)

Not all of us live. A Garry oak falls in its forest
to the hum of horrible feedback. Head Two cuts it
down in some fierce jaws. Buzz and roar of
Demon Husqvarna = young music, lips clapping.

**I read that Garry knew it would soon fall. Garry
once saw a marten limp up doing tricks, slippery
slip from Garry's slick branches. Marten's thud death
≠ Garry's fault. Marten's bloated body at the roots,**

**rain working marten fur ≠ Garry's fault. Garry planned
a death with sequoia dust on saw teeth in its
belly while back and forth the sawyers reaped.**
Chill. Bring the oak down with our simple felling ropes.

**Garry wants to go like its father, who — in an Oregon
forest, a little bird told Garry — was dismantled gently
with handsaw to top branches first.** See how thick
a timber breeds. Unfair play, forward pinch, a tug to slow

death down. Last acts of slow strength. Lumber. **Garry's
pith so soft, green.** Head Two bites, works the trunk
back for slack, as the oak's bowels spit. Husqvarna
monstermouth takes oak to mulch. Head Two reads

death in something named season. **Fall was relief for Garry.
Garry dropped leaves each fall. How am I taking Garry
back through each of his falls? Is Garry glass when he
finally stops fighting? What does mourn = ?, mule deer?**

β Bracatus Majoris: Arbor

The Super Duper gives no guffs for our sacred

Yggdrasils or gizmos. Our land was just a zone where ancient

carrot fields were engineered to cemetery ash in the

Super Duper's wake. A bullpen of reverends volunteered to

lead us to a tamer coded hell. Stocked the place with

hymns and sex robots. Dad volunteered to go, tricked

mom right down in that hole. When sunset hit, both mom

and machines peaced up to save the planet. *Look back*,

Dad begged, as if to write himself Eurydice-knows-best.

Some nights, moonlight roughcasts new neural networks

on our catacombs and walks of fame. Stay above the horizon,

where the diabolists now face our unknown guest.

There is no rest, no visitation, no sign, no signal.

Point up, not down. Invent new answers. Now pitch.

Head Three (Oceans)

Head Three drinks oceans, ransacks our secret formula: $NaCl + H_2O$.
Head Three catches the drift of our slang.
your view from the moon is gonzo...ler nasa, baby.

Ebb and flow is obsolete.
Ten-Headed Alien needs no words for the scars it leaves.
No fangs, no talons and no good docs on our rock.
The world's out-consumed, a wormhole back to its own orifice, like a
      human centipede stitched solo.
our data snitched that you were fun, friends. come play, homeboys.

Strong meat is always guzzled first.
Our promises and plans fuck us.
A senator with a B.Sc. (Zoology) says,
      Poison the oceans: reinvent acid rain.
      Choke Head Three by filling oceans with batteries, old cellular silicon.

In our back pocket, we plot to live *sans* salt water.
We're coolio to constant thirst.
we're coolio without your nacl + H₂0, but do it most def anyway, dude.

Islands pop up in appropriated costumes of opportunity.
Shore borders blur the sand where vacation babies crawled.
A raft is no salvation.
A rocket is no salvation.
We'll race Atlantic in search of Promised Land.
Head Three made a desert out of Margaritaville.
We have a new def of marooned with vistas of Utopia, where oceans once
      soothed or stung our anus so we felt that we bled there.
Our language is worthless, organic, plastic, lonely.
Now I see treasures, trash and bodies at the bottom of No More Ocean.
your anatomies = juice.

Our anatomy was juice.
Crisis appeared in soft breeze, tsunamis are earthquake-common.
Last words litter the beach.
Love letters clog the Mariana Trench and choke the vents.
What does Lonely =, homeboy?

We'll survive without oceans.
We can cope with lakes and all the words for loss.
Picture the globe without blue.
The first map was a brown map: Pangaea throwback.
Maybe I could hide in the sky.

γ Bracatus Majoris: Oceanus

Ignore the minefield of crabs and queens and

twins and dragons – ignore strange slayers on mystery science

hunts. There are machine-driven myths under other suns

that don't evolve our epics. White magic, black ops,

our books of spells and talismans have made off in the

night with our power bars. And so we wail, "Gather now."

Gather in the workshops for parley. Assemble our

three remaining cutthroats for pursuit of the Super Duper.

Reconcile the plan's lack of good crescendo inventory:

no battering rams or trebuchets, no arquebus,

caliver, scareware or gunpowder. No bayonet, no howitzer,

no knife or nuke. No Trojan horse, no froggy potions. Assign our trio

to the sky's soft labyrinth. Sell them up, one by one, with

primal hopes and aluminum arms. Let no human risk the Super Duper.

Head Four (Fresh Water)

It's me. Is anyone left? I have contributed zilch
while Head Four lapped the rivers, lakes and
streams. I haven't heard the voice for about a half
an orbit. It was light years thirstier than we thought.
We proposed our own Ten-Headed Alien to no avail.

Make a machine to match! Queen took bishop. Kong
took Godzilla into the Pacific. So engineer an equal
to our fear. Play it scare jargon. We've gone so ugly,
girls and boys. I boiled my piss, drank it. I lied back,
wished for rain under cadaver white clouds. My brain

is fake Buddhist, and can't hold my weak meditations:
stop sweating. There's water left in my blood, so I try
a great mouth-trick, sucking straight from veins via
puncture from my tooth. I dream of junkies kissing
Doctor Feelgoods. Bless you, girls and boys. Sneeze
in my mouth. Nourish me with a life bringing snot. I'd

believe in holy water if I could guzzle it. Drink proud
at grey water, stoup and sewer. Ahhhhh from a catch
basin. I want to suck the blood from your cuts before
they scab. So, bless my body. Blessblessbless. Goddamn
you, Great Lakes. My memory is a whip's lash: toes,
dock dipping on rocky bottomed Fishtail. Goddamn Baikal,

Titicaca, Nipissing and Okeechobee. All of them gone.
Great Bear, Great Slave, Chad, Ladoga. I would kill a man
for a bottle of Aquafina. Hand-painted signs with lake names
make sense now. They were babies, face it. We were addicts,
jonesin' and a next world conflict withdrew a freshwater fix.
And what does junkie =, David? Please let me sleep

without pike-visions, one I nabbed on Falcon Lake. I let
the slimy dragon go. Set it swimming with the hook in its lip.
Please let me go. There's enough to nightmares at our newfangled
deserts. I don't even ask you for drink or mercy. If precincts
still logged cause of death, the scrolls would read *Osmosis*.

ε Bracatus Majoris: Lacus

Call forth Lacus a Hunter. Make him lead with

virtual reality bow – campfire carved of locust branch,

the knots metal-scraped smooth. Behold, Lacus's arrow tips

of poison ivy, dipped in antifreeze, with pheasant feather fletches.

We write his weapon's romance viral: a primitive hunter,

killer, crackerjack with a land-scavenged tool, with

Love tattooed across his right knuckles, with

Hate tattooed across his left. Look down, Lacus.

There are weapons in this junk. The gritstone is a weapon.

Creekside willow is a weapon. Our smartphone entrails are weapons.

Vow, Lacus – go pierce the Super Duper with earth and polymer.

Don't come back without the Super Duper's heads – or the story

of the beheadings. Tell us of the bloodshot eyes

when sharpened transistor took the weight from its back.

Head Five (Beauty)

From Pacifist Grotto down in Coward's Steppe, I spot the fifth head at all
 horizons, and it vocal wails, **you're a scared boy, now!**

Our mouths are slack-jawed face-caves at the base of ex-avalanches,
 chins in the mud, the deadbeat flash floods never come.

Head Five Fosbury flops skyward, plucks rainwater from the clouds,
 wet meat ghosts from a soft grey bone.

Head Five shovels snow from Rockies to Alps, circumnavigates the peaks
 to twin them with the dry sucked valleys.

Why didn't we telethon to mine clouds – *drill, nimbostratus Baby, drill* –
 in days of cute and cozy droughts?

We wasted billions building domes for baseball teams.

We fixed holes in the roof where the rain got in.

Some of us are left, right?

Head Five bulges larger than the rest. Survivor premise: design symmetry,
 resource allocation, efficiency of a big brain centre-set.

Living scientists attribute anatomy to hydrocephalus, refusing sportsmanship
 of compliment. We won't see greatness in our conquer.

I forget what life beyond biology is.

Meh. Maybe I'm the lint that's left, no rain to wash me, no crowds to
 drown in.

ζ Bracatus Majoris: Pulchritudo

Call forth, Pulchritudo the hunter, carting bronze pots of boiling water

to stew the beast then dole meat back to its human victims.

Feed us the Super Duper's power, Pulchritudo. Grow your pot

strong with alloys from our galaxy elements:

platinum, rhodium, ruthenium in your spine. Each tear dropped

left us less precious human salts with which to build you.

Our blood iron shrunk from star to vein to burial plot.

You get what's left. The sky betrayed like sepsis, like our data.

In a cruel lab, alchemists churn out new star patterns and titrate curses

into vials. But Vow, Pulchritudo! Stoke a fire beneath the catch.

Burn the Super Duper's shell to smithereens, transmit the smell

of your win down from the exosphere, that pungent burn of sulphur

from the Super Duper's flesh will be creature comfort. Our universe is a

molecule made on the fly. Broadcast the coup from the distance between us.

Head Six (War)

The wars: we're drawn to them
as if in fever, we sleepwalk to them
wake up in full stride of nightmare,
blood slippery, mouth deep in their gore.

– Jim Harrison, "War Suite"
(examined: small paper, burned edges, a doomed fighter's pocket)

Head Six scans history for feigned retreats.
Our military thinks strategy stores
in Head Six's vault, its gaze perusing panzer
tanks and *The Art of War*. we've read your life.
you've got no surprises left, so mute your
call for ambush, for battle drum, friends,
ship us your generals for execution, stat!
Our generals surrender, promising it was
a pleasure to lead. They won't condemn
the wars: we're drawn to them,

so we retell the great battles, sneaking
hints from war poems and Hollywood. Egypt's
resurrection at Megiddo, the Romans
rout at Pydna. Caesar at Pharsalus
beheading a Republic. Summon those
spirits: myths of Saladin, Patton, Nelson,
Uncle Isaac and Tecumseh arriving
deus ex machina on their horses. Hold
tight for legends. It isn't legend's end.
As if in fever, we sleepwalk to them,

and return to doctrine on the curdled
front. Scan for redemption endings
in the *I Ching*. Send believers to Job's tomb
on a Dhofar hill. Plop ascetics beneath lotus
trees missed by Head Two. Resurrect the
godly ways by rocks of former waterfalls.
Mash Zoroaster's golden rule and Voltaire's
best possible worlds. Stretch Zen and Zion.
Deify lost lakes and fire, the hajj and prayer.
Wake up in full stride of nightmare

when we're pinched studying these oldies.
We've fed the enemy secrets, downloaded
our aggregate's theology porn. We're pages
now, battle tactics scanned by the hostile.
Belief was a blind stab. We doubted alien
existence. Now we're flanked by a oneness.
Moon with a face. The simplicity of a centaur
would be a breather. Which head took you
from me? Friends, assembly is an act of war.
Blood slippery, mouth deep in their gore.

η Bracatus Majoris: Bellum

Get in the ring, Bellum the Hunter. Follow Pulchritudo,

bring firewood to keep the fire belligerent.

Where you're going, there's no O_2 to keep the flame

a-breathin'. Innovate to solve that restrictive law of fire.

Melt the Super Duper's bone carbon. Bleed it

of its toxic marrow. Stain water sanguine with streaks

from Lacus's arrows, the heat from Pulchritudo's pot.

In concert, your intelligence is bass and drum and vocals.

The primus of our freedom. Make salvation palatable.

Season, gut and butcher! Close the gap in the Super Duper's

head start. Permission for each sin experiment activated.

Your fingernails committing wrath. A gluttonous bite you take from

the Super Duper's hump. Sell swagger in deliverance.

Spit swear: we owe you stars. Your names will roll from tongues.

Head Seven (Thought)

This is not Head One. This is Head Seven. I have been here
all along and deserve some credit. I can read your thoughts.

You think they're still your thoughts, but I am tinkering with
your limbic bits. You hear me the way you heard memory.

My voice is truer than the one you called *inner*. If my vibration
is scarier than Head One's racket, then you're still sane. Kudos.

I know the facts you consider yourself. Your world's progress,
your science, made this puzzle a snap. The exoplanet in what

you called Cygnus was not a straight line. It took an exoplanet,
in what you called Proxima Centauri, two years to relent in full.

Some worlds evolve on a parabola. I just use your secrets against
you. I know the art you wanted to invent. We found the songs

you tried to hide, but you know they are eventually nothing
against us. We extracted dictators you wish you still had. I know

the problem of your art and am hard at work on how to solve
it. Impressive if you could mobilize. I know what your easy stories

mean. We keep these themes from Head Eight, of course. Yes,
we can cauterize as you did. We can share our body in places

your adrenalin and cortisol would have you hotfot. I know a few
of you still forage for our weakness with your language,

that you've diagnosed Head Eight. I share this with you because
we're in the next phase of our presence. Exoplanet KOI-7711

came close to defending itself with abstract cannons, but we've
yet to lose. The noise you try won't drown my suggestion. I know

you've been restless. I knew your thirtysomething insomnia.
Squirming with coin flips, four a.m. and wondering if you were

in the right bed. You worried about $$$ and mortality. You were
paralyzed on a metronome's tock. Your muscles are not bored

by the limo wreck of your planet. Be honest. You once regretted
your free time. You jotted milestones on napkins, scratched light

bulbs in book margins. *Live in a van. Live in Greece. Learn
sheet music.* Your parties skipped tremor. Yet you're alive, and I want

to tell you that I haven't solved you yet. You. Yes, you, David.
Don't think it's a sign of your superior intelligence. It's just, you

lie to yourself so fucking much. Even now, you think of the past
as a poorly used calendar. Even now, you think my voice is you

going batshit, not my cranks on your amygdala. Smell the grass
clippings . . . but do you see any grass here? Just think if you had studied

us – not yourself in a mirror. Turned your leisure into force field.
Turned your *I* into *Us*. Protested ego and endocrine system. You

think you're lonely, but you have me now, friend. An earworm is
the only worm we let live. I'm showing you a tunnel in. Trace

your hand against its walls. Trace your hand against its walls.
Trace your hand against its walls.

δ Bracatus Majoris: Quamquam

We look to the stars where others tweet their prayers,

and in a blink some 4.54 billion years passes by in a day

in the sky. Blink. 13.8 billion years. Blink. And still,

our trio follows by night, sleeps by sunrise, while the Super Duper

eludes, bobs, survives, weaves, but is chased from our

community across the big bright arc. We've breathed new cities

in this time beneath the twinkle of retreat – our hunters

at the Super Duper's butt. Lacus   and his weapon

then Pulchritudo   and his weapon   then Bellum and

his weapon. That constant line of hunters trailing the

Super Duper's ass. A chase so steady that the hunters have

become the tail the alien never had. Now we know, of course, that no

hybrid could have ever done shit against the Super Duper,

that we launched three suckers for the good of the bunch.

Head Eight (Emotion)

Head Eight tickle-picks at our ingredients like we're
Arcimboldo heads; hair of snake den, our eyes
dwarf planets backlit by full moons. Head Eight
probes our theme, hears the heartbeat's clock noise,
laughter's waltz upon the jilted. Head Eight wants
to know the ways we're lonely. It's in hiding too.
Head Eight curio-sniffs in libraries and theatres,
whiffs echoes in the vacuums. Head Eight copies
Rodin's pensive posture, thinks, *When can I be bronze?*
     Ladies and gentleman. We got 'em.

Kandinsky on our shields. Turn outs in Bauhaus school
flak jackets. Head Eight is hypnotized by Dada-flesh,
tattoos from head to toe. Head Eight won't strike shelters
splattered Pollock, is a kitten at Rothko lines, spies
its future in Caravaggio's decapitated Goliath.

We bloat the arsenal by genres: Schoenberg is a bullet.
Virginia Woolf is a bullet. King Crimson, Abramović
and Chikamatsu are bullets.

I sneak a few numb laughs during this duck-under.
It's intermission, and our relief roots where
the water lilies used to.
Salud! To those artists who promised their shit could be
a change agent. Most of our choir is long dead, but we have
flat champagne for toasts. *To the vindicated! To the castrated!*

Under a Van Gogh sky's banal swirls
of cobalt blue and Indian yellow, Head Eight and I share
a little hamartia. *I met our last hopes once, Head Eight.*
I believe that the artists I knew lived forever-fighting.

Huhtanen, Latosik and Aisha Sasha John. D'Agostino,
Jenn Nichols, Couture and Di Genova. Fight on:
Hood and Ming, Gareth Williams, the clean heart of Omie.
Head Eight and I were always
Krakatoa magma in your palms.

Fight on, child and conjurer and genius, you bullets.
I dig a tear from Head Eight's head. Let me drink
from that eye, friend. Let me drink from the moon we share.
We both know tonight is temporary.

o Bracatus *Majoris*: Perturbatio

And we can program a constellation of anything, now.

The hunt's journey dissolved from our groupthink,

and vanished in the fifth wave's distance. That story of the

clergy in graveyards can be locked up in a book, or bastardized

in a drunk retelling – old plagues help us pipe out the rats.

Binary is the best of a people's epidemics. Software translates nouns,

erases contexts. Truths and stars die in dense double suicides,

climaxes so antediluvian that no one stands to witness the Thunderbird

drive into the canyon. We can craft a ray gun from a cipher and a bad idea.

We made atom bombs from notions. Our booby traps are principle-based.

Pooh-pooh old quests, that slow race to the moon. Those bodies hang

over us for less than half a day. No biggie. They shuffle off.

Our reverence is sylphlike. We cobbled folklore from

the whole shebang. We're hotshots at them-there myths.

Head Nine (Action)

Head Nine is twin star, takes the shape of whatever looks
at the fucking thing. I saw my face for the last time on Nine.
A bear sees a bear and an ant sees an ant, if an ant would look.

The inquisitive face of apes should've clued us in on viewing
unknowns at first contact. each of you are subjects.
we're all in this together now. Here is what we want

from those still here. we want you to destroy us. It's
why we come to homes like yours. Head Nine knows why
the elephant tilts its head. Head Nine knows why Eight

was decapitated and discarded in the Arctic desert. even now,
you worry your bullshit is too simple, don't you, David?
Our enemies reflect what we really were. Mismatched,

jelly, expert destroyer, perfect fumbler. I wanted a happy
end to this trip. There were flutes and clichés planned
for the coda. Not panic brine in test tubes, spilled milk

on the cutting-room roots. We must've been weak and strong,
or the Ten-Headed Alien would've been empty. At long last,
our worst failures were simply self-copies. Atychiphobia is

that fear of failure. Just see your weakness, and see it
on nine. we'd quit then. We looked for strength, but it's
a flywheel for thing's power. Mistakes spun that turbine.

We see our offer on the horizon, or in the last breath of life.
The images mimic potential, hand at the brow where we'd
squint for sunsets, star showers, blue moons and each other.

Super moons and each other. Blood moons and each other.
see us as something you can destroy. see us as yourselves.
Take your planet back, or even I have failed this mission.

ι Bracatus Majoris: Actio

Our terror was real, then robot, then myth, now amnesia.

Our crew can live beneath that shape.

Paint symbols of salvation on faith-based

ceilings. We can trick ourselves that ceilings are

a sky full of satellites. So we go on. History so far

out of range we call it fantasy. Our conspiracy shooed heroes on a

goose chase, so the air would feel no heat from

wild giants and their plots. It's all up there. The huffs and puffs of the

Super Duper and our hunters are now pretty glints in a

clear night sky. Look up. Three imaginations chased the Super Duper

as stooges always do. Look closer, they could never have caught it.

See the roof on tonight's chapel? Its monsters, its swirling

VIPs, its wild creatures with their backs turned? See the distance

we've put between ourselves   and the end of the world.

Head Ten (Diplomacy)

Head Ten slept through it all,
January's hibernating griz. A torpor,

and our side won. We have their voice now.
The loser collected all our secrets in its

bladder bag, but not all wars end in truce.
Was this even war for them? The last victims

thought of stealing heroes from the sky, but
all that's left is ruins, rodents. They had silly phrases

like *bat out of hell* and *bull in a china shop*.
We go now as conquerors, make collage from their scrap.

We'll write this first poem for the world we
now own. We will try out their language,

approach their metalwork. We'll do so much
better with their tools. Our voice is louder than

our conscience, and we think this song will do
despite a quiet ending –

crescendo, vocal wail, abrupt end, no coda.

The Ruins *(23:04)*

a. Morning Prayer Recited by Head One (2:25)

History is a victor's party.
Years ago, something lived here very much like a thing called dinosaur.
Do not mourn the artefacts.
The mission has always been to make the best of current hosts who could
    not make us better.
We learned from their people to speak this way.
We told them they would not be hurt, but they never believed in the things
    they saw or heard, so they we hurt very much.
They fired medicine and weapons, music and prayers.
Most of the mess we clean up is their defence.
Our nature is a solitary power, but do not call it lonely.
Let each of your heads work with that knowledge, young ones.
Never forget, we were not here first.
Never forget, your eighth head cannot lead you.
You must be prepared to remove the weak parts of yourself.
Keep your tenth head asleep.
Something else could come ... look up ... something out there.
Something we cannot imagine.
Something so very much like us, and we must not embrace pity.

b. Artefact Carved in the Bark of Garry the Glass Tree (Undiscovered) (3:10)

Save us. If u r reading this,
and the trees aren't ground to sand,
if there are still windows and walls,
if the lens of the eye isn't exiled
we r hiding
in the (ILLEGIBLE)
– DB + (ILLEGIBLE)

c. The New Map Replaced the Old Map, but the Old Map is Collectible Memory (0:54)

dust and tan, puce, no blue.
khaki, umber, no green, nut.
ochre, ecru, beige, just brown.
dust and tan, puce, no blue.

d. Skeletal Remains at the Bottom of Former Fishtail Lake (Discovered) (1:57)

Palatable skeleton: no depth of fat, no extra few, no baggy eyes or yellow swell, no organ pain, no varicose vein, no acrid breath or fungal bumps. Grown full, shed as branches of a winter tree on timeless white. In flesh, so much missed – the confidence of an adult jaw cut; the spunky, angry youth revives in a skinless point, old politics. That framework once poked at ingrown hair, lamented each mole, against each freckle and spot as a failure. Now the crooked assembly of each curl accuses the body of weeping far too often to be called alive. There were too many opportunities for our defeated to hate how the mandible moved, the sad rooms entered on their metatarsals, what they hid under sternum and rib.

e. Paper Hidden in a Plastic Bottle on the Top of Mount Olympus (Undiscovered) (3:51)

I should be searching for food and water, for other people, but I have given up on a saviour. I resisted pessimism until it kicked me in the nuts. Even so, I promise I want to live, so if you are reading this, keep looking. No one would have believed the story of what we became. It was too impossible and familiar. The stuff of pulp, not poems. Had I decided to write it, it would've been a movie, but who would've bought it? My last piece of paper records my fear of failure. If I eat it, I will live another day, but erase that I was here. Find me if you can. Bring water or blood if you have it.

f. No Myths Left Unplundered (Discovered Etched in a Cave) (1:17) g. The Once Popular Sci-Fi Music Genre (Recording Found) (2:48)

But What Did Their Skin Look Like?
Poem for a Mellotron

Like fine bones of long-dead fish placed on dried-
out cobs of corn, kernels eaten at an outdoor

dinner on a bygone Earth. I expected black organs
through a lucent shell, space druids, a rushing plasma

revealing similarities between our species. I remember
a sound on the skin, a wonderful hum that told me

I was about to be taken. The skin played music
in notes mostly like the ones we have. I did not see

bright light. It happened like pond fog. My thoughts
turned banal: the leftovers in my fridge, I knew I wasn't

about to die. (Is that oddball?) The abduction was hot –
but you asked about their skin. I was off to be

a curiosity. (Maybe there'd be pain.) They were limbless.
I could teach them of hands. Maybe they'd learn

mercy. I promised I wouldn't fight back. I smelled
an ease of relenting: a flower with petals I can't

name, having no botany in the brain tank. Believe me,
I gave up quickly. I thought I'd feel flight, but I sank

somewhere. Nothing else in my time as captive remains.
Sorry I can't tell you more. You ask me what I do

remember. My first fear was hunger, not their skin
of dried corn ... fishbones. On Earth, we could eat them

as deterrence. Now, since everyone I knew is gone,
please tell me which year I've returned to.

h. Head Eight Hid One Private Memory Stolen from a Defeated (Contraband) (2:51)

and it finds me. I am hidden in
laundry that will never be clean.

Eight studies me, looks back as
if someone is coming.

It nudges me gently. It is
the last living thing I'll touch.

Eight curls around me. A bear
hug, somehow I feel loved. We sit together

this way for hours; I am cradled,
while I hum the quiet song I wrote

for you. This is a slow dance, a singalong.
Head Eight's voice is a click of a

tongue made electric. The vibration of
a guitar put down after a solo. Its cheek

rubs mine. This tells me, it is both our
last night with a feeling like this.

It is at this point I begin to
think of myself as exceptional,

and not because I am the
last one left.

i. Atychiphobia (Their memories are weather. It rains a lot.) (2:01)

I don't   want to   fight back. I don't   want to   be lonely,
        but   I'm   lonely. The   wrath is infinite.   There was
            snow swirling on a rooftop once.   Now nothing
    is cold.   There is no cold.   All that matters is that
    feeling of cold.   Everything prevented everything
    and   now   there are no   barriers.

    It's dark and
there is   nothing   and even imagination can
        be created from the   elements left in the sky.
        It could rain again,
but   that'd   take   so   much   time.

j. We Go Now (1:51)

CRESCENDO
The climax, then the cliff, chasing rest note after rest note.

VOCAL WAIL
The Wilhelm scream was a fiction, repeated often enough to become common
    last words.

ABRUPT END
There are tin cans on shelves deep in bunkers that will someday be fossils.

NO CODA
I ate paper and metal. I'd evolve in this lifetime. I was wrong, so it ends.

ACKNOWLEDGEMENTS

I gratefully acknowledge the editors of the following publications for including early versions of these poems in their pages: *The Puritan*, *Maisonneuve*, *This Magazine*, the *Dusie* blog, *NewPoetry*, the Sunrise with Sea Monsters project and the 2017 Inaugural Poem Project.

Thanks to Dani Couture, Jeff Latosik, Andrew Faulkner, ol' Winnipeg Jon Brown, Carla Huhtanen, Gareth Williams, Jennifer Nichols and Ciaran Hanrahan-Powers for your gifts of reading, conversation, feedback and inspiration.

I'm indebted to Ingrid Paulson for this Roger Dean–esque prog rock book design.

Thank you to the team at Wolsak & Wynn, especially Noelle Allen and Ashley Hisson, for trusting me with a second collection, and to the magnificent Paul Vermeersch, whose belief in me as a poet keeps demanding that I become one.

Continued love to my parents and sister, Stangie and Jill, for their unending support and wisdom.

And as always, intergalactic love to Erin for all the strange magic.

NOTES

"Bionic Pigeon Wing on the Roadside" won first place in the 2017
Ontario Book Publishers Organization's What's Your Story?
competition (Etobicoke), appearing in the anthology of the same
name. Thanks to OBPO.

"the little punks have always counted" is after a speech from Frank
Capra's *Meet John Doe* (1941).

"Jake, Damien, Soft, Tender" is for Will Kemp and Spencer Gordon.

"Disco's Out, Murder's In" is the title of a 1990 Suicidal Tendencies song.

Portions of the Bracatus Majoris poems originally appeared as a
monologue from my play *Centre of the Universe* (Theatre Lab, 2014).
Thanks to Michael Orlando and Omie Syphu for your input on the text.

"The Ruins" structure is based on Van der Graaf Generator's song
"A Plague of Lighthouse Keepers" from the 1971 album *Pawn Hearts*.
Obviously.

"No Myths Left Unplundered (Discovered Etched in a Cave) (1:17)"
was co-created by Paul Vermeersch and David James Brock.

David James Brock is a playwright, poet and librettist whose plays and operas have been performed in cities across Canada, the US and the UK. He is the winner of the 2011 Herman Voaden Canadian National Playwriting Award for his play *Wet*. Brock's debut poetry collection, *Everyone is CO2*, was released by Wolsak & Wynn in spring 2014. He has created text for opera and new music with companies that include Scottish Opera, NOISE, Tapestry Opera, the Canadian Art Song Project, FAWN Chamber Collective and the Paul Dresher Ensemble. Brock is co-creator of *Breath Cycle*, a multimedia operatic song cycle developed with cystic fibrosis patients that was nominated for a 2014 Royal Philharmonic Society Music Award. He lives in Toronto and has taught writing courses at the University of Guelph, University of Victoria, Humber College and Young People's Theatre. Learn more about his work at www.davidjamesbrock.com.